AF321959

DARK CODE

Think beyond limits

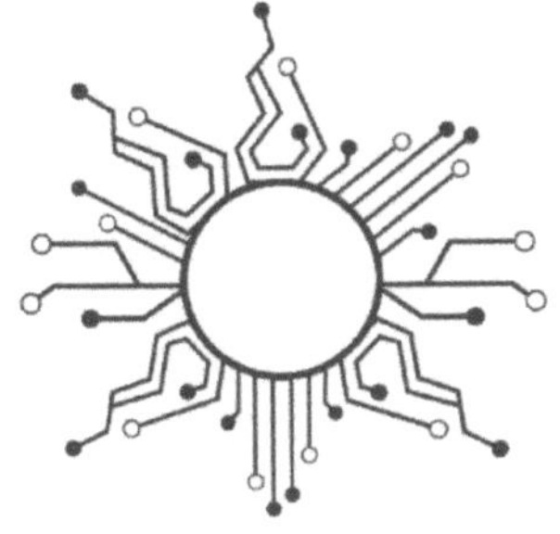

Published By

www.poetryworld.org

Dark Code

Written By Keshav Joshi

Published by: Poetry World Org.

Publisher's Address: Haryana

All rights are reserved. No part of this publication may be reproduced, stored in a retrieval system, or transmitted, in any form or by any means, electronic, mechanical, photocopying, recording or otherwise, without the prior written permission of the publisher. The author asserts the moral right to be identified as the author of this work. Special credits to Dr.Niveditha and Dr.Nitin Chopra.

Edition: I (2021)

ISBN (Paperback) - 9789390724918

Book Design by POETRY WORLD

Copyright © Keshav Joshi

POETRY WORLD ORG 2021

DARK CODE

Think beyond limits

Keshav Joshi

Software Engineer, ON Canada

ABOUT THE BOOK

"Think beyond limits", as it says, when the problem cannot be countered within the boundaries, logic needs to exceed the limits. Dark Code, discusses the data confidentiality measures i.e., Steganography and Cryptography. Cryptograph is the process of changing the form of data in order to achieve confidentiality whereas, Steganography is the art of hiding data inside media carriers without changing its form. The prime focus of this book is to explain how steganography works, what are the fallouts of this art and their countermeasures. Direct manipulation of pixels inside images, sure gives the advantage of negligible suspicion to the native eye, but this approach itself invites the biggest downside of this art as well. There are numerous pixel manipulation techniques i.e., compression, encryption, etc. that can distort the payload and it is totally irrecoverable.

When it comes to the countermeasures, this book demonstrates the step algorithm that preserves the payload under the direct pixel manipulation attacks. Moreover, this book accentuates the alpha, its importance of controlling opacity in the image and a proposed technique to implement steganography using alpha value. The term "Fusion" has been introduced, which refers to concealing an image inside another image, and how this methodology is different from steganography. The idea of this book was to reassemble the ancient art of steganography in a way that has never been discussed before. The described methods are the standards of how a very significant value inside an image can be so productive and how the data can be modified in different ways to implement the general principle.

ABOUT THE AUTHOR

Keshav Joshi is a computer science engineer currently working as a Software Developer in Toronto. Joshi, completed his Bachelor's from Lovely Professional University, India and has done his Post Graduation Diploma from Centennial College, Canada. Keshav Joshi has a major interest in research and development. He has a wide range of skillsets and has command over numerous programming languages. Joshi, has experience working in finance, IT and embedded industries. He has a prime inclination towards mobile and web applications and has published several applications over years. Joshi has also worked on concepts like augmented reality and machine learning along with other industry standards.

Keshav Joshi developed a new technique in the field of steganography and his research paper was published in IJERT (International Journal of Engineering Research and Technology), 2018. The prime focus of the paper was to maximize the payload (secret data) capacity by eliminating the visual disorders that can be detected by the native eye. His paper received more than 10 citations globally and is listed under some renowned scholarly literature search engines i.e., Google Scholar and Semantic Scholar. He recently launched his own website www.keshavjoshi.com, where all of his work, projects and research is being displayed.

"To my parents,

who helped me exceeding my own limits"

PREFACE

I, Keshav Joshi, am a computer science engineer and am majorly interested in research and development. It all started with an interest in manipulating image pixels and before I could have realized it, my interest turned into a passion and I started analyzing the solutions for hiding data inside pixels. The aim of this research was to discuss the delightful techniques of steganography under direct manipulation attacks and how efficiently the value of alpha can be used to implement steganography. Moreover, the term Fusion was introduced in this study and how it stands a different place than steganography.

By moving further, I would like to thank my parents, who taught me the value of life and motivated me to keep pushing myself beyond limits. Moreover, I'm very thankful to my mentor Mr.Roshan Srivastava for his continuous support and expertise, which helped me to become what I'm today. I would also like to express my gratitude towards Mr. Majura Maheswaran, who trusted me with my abilities and gave a kickstart to my career.

Although this book is intended mainly for those who are interested in steganography and those who want to get insights into this field, I really hope that it will meet the expectations of all the readers who are interested in computer science. The algorithmic approach is specifically accentuated to gain the interests of logical thinkers and learners. The term steganography is very vast and it involves multidimensional terminologies. Considering this fact, this book is written from a very specific point of view. At last, I would like to pay my greetings to those who helped me and motivated me in any way in order to get this study done.

TABLE OF CONTENTS

CHAPTER -1 INTRODUCTION

Data plays a very crucial role in today's network. All the analysis, observations, and probabilities are based upon data enumeration. With this characteristic development, factors like confidentiality and integrity of data needs to be looked upon with caution. There are numerous ways, by which, this can be achieved, but cryptography and steganography are the most important ones. Cryptography is the science of authenticating data by changing its form. The process of changing the data form is called encryption and its reverse is called decryption. There are a variety of strong encryption algorithms available that helps serve the purpose. For example, DES, AES, SHA-256, SHA-51, etc. On the other hand, Steganography is the art of concealing data within other media carriers without changing its form. In computer science a text, image, and a video is concealed within another text, image, and video.

In this book, we're discussing

steganographic principles, their working and most importantly, some uncommon techniques. In steganography, its effectiveness depends upon the media carriers. If the encrypted media transmits through any kind of compression, steganography fails. It is owing to the fact that all the markers inside the media are lost, and this loss is not recoverable. Hence, this is where steganography lacks behind cryptography. "Dark Code" as the name suggests, contains some delightful techniques and algorithms that overcome this flaw, up to a certain extent i.e., techniques that let encrypted media pass through compression and still manage to retrieve the data. It is important to know that, the productivity of these algorithms is equivalent to, how they are used. Some standard approaches are being discussed, but they can be extended to a higher level of efficiency. Moreover, an interesting method has also been discussed to hide data inside images using alpha value by aiming maximum payload capacity. Alpha is the prime focus of this book because of its ability to control opacity. The concept of fusion is introduced in this book. Fusion is defined as the merging of two images together and retrieving back the same results. It is a different concept from steganography as the encoded image gets distorted by the process, but the end results are lossless.

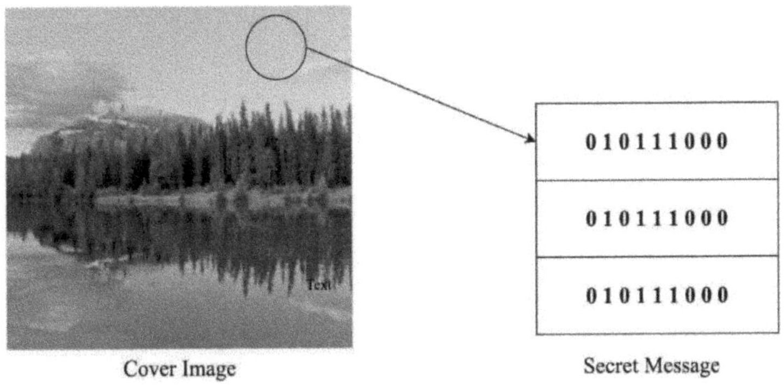

Figure 1 Image showing Steganography

CHAPTER – 2 STEGANOGRAPHY

Steganography is the art of secure transmission of messages from a sender to a receiver by hiding message inside different media carries like images, videos, audios etc. The main purpose of this technique is to achieve confidentiality and security. It is a very ancient technique, as it can be traced back to 1499 when the term was originally introduced by Johannes Trithemius in his book. From the use of invisible ink between the visible lines to the use of digital media, Steganography has evolved in a tremendous way and can be categorized into different domains.

2.1   Spatial Domain Methods

This domain refers to the cover image itself and involves the direct manipulation in some bits of the pixel values. There are various versions of spatial steganography, but Least Significant Bit

(LSB) is the very common technique with no encryption and no compression in this domain. LSB hides a secret message in the pixel values without many perceptible distortions. Hence, immensely drop the chances of images getting suspected for secret messages and increase data security. Moreover, payload capacity is very calculated, as data is getting stored directly in the pixels. This approach is preferable when a cover image cannot be compromised over pixel distortion and a large amount of data needs to be hidden. On the other hand, there is a downfall to this technique, as it is not very robust. The secret message can be easily lost by tampering pixels and might not be recoverable. Any compression medium and encryption algorithm can result in a total loss.

- **Least Significant Bit**

Image is a collection of pixels arranged in a grid manner. Each pixel consists of three numeric values i.e., red, green and blue, each range between 0-255.

In this approach, each bit of red, green, and blue value is modified. Therefore, in total 3 pixels or 8 bits are required to store 1 byte, and similarly, 8 megabyte of image is required to store 1 megabyte of data. Since, the change of the last bit in pixel values is not a visually perceptible change to the native eye, a person observing the original and modified image, won't be able to point out a difference.

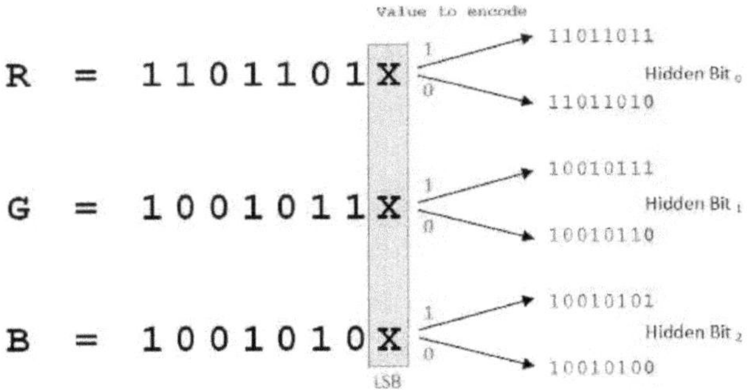

Figure 2 Least Significant Bit

Here, 8 bytes are denoted to 1 byte of data, so therefore, total number of pixels divided by 8 gives the maximum payload capacity. Payload capacity defines the amount of data that can be concealed in a given media. This method can be optimized further to increase the payload capacity by decreasing the intensity of pixels so that the PSNR ratio remains equivalent and changes cannot be visually noticed. This approach is explained in the International Journal of Engineering Research and Technology.[1]

2.2   Transform Domain Methods

This method is a bit complex and advanced way of data hiding. Unlike, directly accessing the pixels to hide data, this approach uses various algorithms and techniques to accomplish the task. The term is referred to as the domain of embedding techniques [2] to which numerous algorithms are available. Today, most steganographic systems operate with transform domain methods. It has a huge advantage over spatial domain methods because this technique hides data in areas that have fewer chances of being exposed to compression and encryption. In other words, transform domain methods are not affected by source manipulation. There are various methods that falls under this domain but the most important ones are Discrete Cosine Transformation (DCT) and Discrete Wavelet Transform (DWT).

- **Discrete Cosine Transform**

This method is applied to cover image in Spatial domain so that it can be converted into frequency domain in which redundancy can be identified. In simple terms, this method applies discrete cosine approach on the spatial domain to get the desired result. When it comes to payload manipulation which results in spatial domain method failures, JPEG is the image format that uses compression to reduce the size. It is single-edged, as the compressed image cannot be retrieved back to its original state, along with the steganographic payload. In JPEG compression, the image is divided into an 8X8 matrix and then the Discrete Cosine Transform (DCT) is applied to each of these 8X8 blocks. After that, by using Least significant Bit (LSB), secret message is hidden at LSBs of DCT coefficients. In the reversal process, Inverse Discrete Cosine Transform (IDCT) is applied to all of these 8X8 blocks.

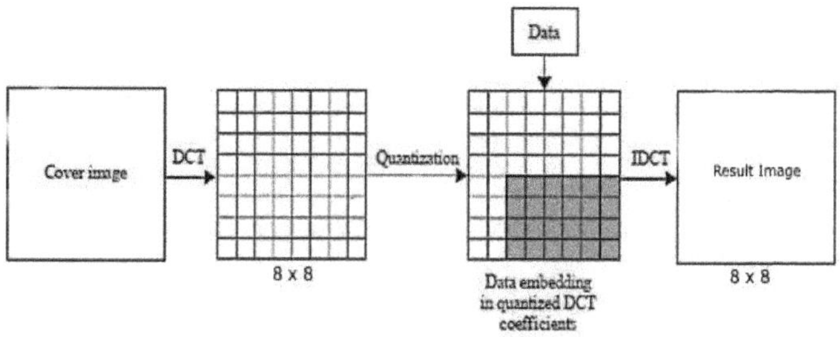

Figure 3 Flow of Discrete Cosine Transform (DCT)

The above diagram [3] elucidates the flow of Discrete Cosine Transform and it's working.

- **Discrete Wavelet Transform**

This is a computationally complex and effective technique. The term wavelet refers to a wave, which oscillates in a time dimension. Wavelet analysis is capable to perform multi-resolution analysis, which is to analyse different frequencies with different resolutions. It is divided into continuous and discrete analysis.

Discrete Wavelet Transform, splits the signal into high and low-frequency parts and generates four bands LL, LH, HL, and HH. The LL band is obtained after passing low-frequency signals to vertical and horizontal directions, which in this case are rows and columns, in order to get the blueprint of an image. The HH band is a high-frequency filtration in both directions, and obtain the high-frequency components along the diagonals [3]. Moreover, as the bands signify, LH and HL are the results of passing low-frequency filtration in one direction and high frequency on the other side. After the image is successfully processed by the DWT, the LL band contains most of the information. Embedding the information in LL makes it unaffected to various pixel manipulation attacks, but can lead to visual noise in the image which increases the suspicion.[4]

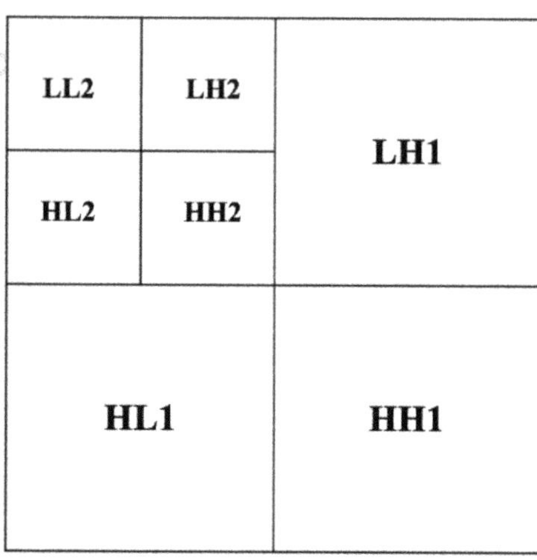

Figure 4 Discrete Wavelet Transform

Algorithm:

- Choose the cover image and image to hide.

- Hide the image using DWT to get the coefficients value.

- Choose one coefficient as the cover image.

- Use the LSB technique to hide the secret image into a cover image

- Reverse the process, in order to get the secret image. The process is called Inverse Discrete Wavelet Transform (IDWT).

27

CHAPTER-3 STEP ALGORITHM

This chapter is the prime focus of this book and discuss about the stepping algorithm and how it works in order to perform steganography. The aim of this approach is to keep the payload unaffected by any pixel manipulation method i.e., encryption and compression. The algorithm is computationally complex and proceeds by converting the spatial domain into the transform domain.

3.1   Working

Encryption:

Let's say there is an image with 'R' number of rows and 'C' number of columns. Firstly, the size of the step needs to be selected. There are numerous ways by which it can be determined, but it is important to note that the larger the value of the step, the more efficient is the output. In this case, the term output means whether the algorithm is able to decrypt the message by reversing the process or not. Below mentioned, a detailed description of how to calculate the step. Furthermore, the pixel values in the cover image are used, to store only a bit from secret bytes. For example,

DARK CODE

$$D = 0 1 0 0 0 1 0 0$$

Figure 5 Binary Conversion

Here, the letter 'D' from 'Dark Code' is converted to an 8-bit binary form, and each bit requires an entire pixel to store its value. Similarly, all the remaining characters are processed. The message can be stored in many other ways, but there is a very specific reason why characters are converted into binary and then those binaries are being stored. It is because of its algorithmic nature. After an image is processed, the pixel value does not just represent the data, in fact, it means its frequency (low or high) as well. It becomes more clearer in the retrieval process of secret message.

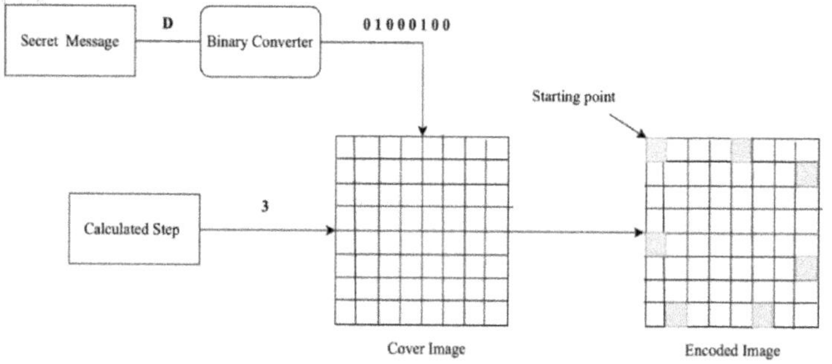

Figure 6 Data Hiding

This technique is very visually distorted as pixel values are replaced by frequencies which is either low or high. In other algorithms, pixel values get modified up to a certain extent so that it does not raise any suspicion, but in this approach pixel values are getting replaced by either 0 or 1 which is definitely a visual hazard. Hence, comes the concept of larger step sizes. Moreover, only edges are used to store the data, because in high-resolution images and high step values, there are fewer chances of distortion to be detected by a native   eye.

Decryption:

In order to decode the secret message, processing begins from the starting point of the image and get all the pixel values that are step value away from the previous one. The result of this would be a binary array. Divide this binary array into sets, each of size 8, and convert these 8-bit binary blocks to respective characters using binary to decimal converter. Repeat this process for the remaining binary blocks and aggregate together the output. If everything goes well without any failure, it will give a hidden secret message.

This is an ideal case of decryption, but would not happen every time. If the cover image goes through any pixel manipulation, the result of traversing pixels might not be a binary array. Therefore, in such a case, if the pixel value is less than the mid-value, it will be considered as low frequency (0) else it will be a high-frequency value (1). There are a total of 256 (0-255) pixel values.

The mid-value would be 127. This is a very efficient approach to deal with JPEG compression over steganography.

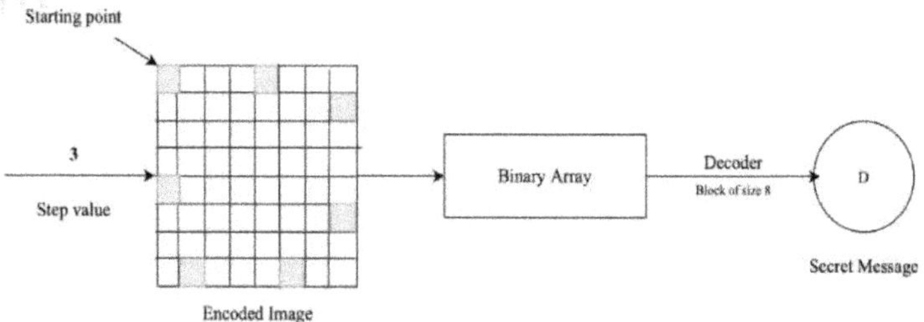

Figure 7 Decoding secret message

Calculate Step Size:

It is the most crucial point of the entire algorithm. Step size has to be as maximum as possible, but at the same time, the entire data needs to be stored among the pixels. Too large a step value might result in some bits being left out which will result in the failure of the reversal process. Therefore, it needs to be calculated and very accurate. It can be calculated with any logic as soon as it follows this algorithm. Here in this chapter, the step value is calculated as follows:

- Find the perimeter of the cover image

- Calculate the total number of bits to be stored.

- Retrieve the remainder of perimeter with total bits as zero

- Divisor of both is the maximum step value it can have.

If the remainder of perimeter and total bits is not zero, then it is very clear that this number of bits cannot be stored in this image. Either the image has to be bigger or the data needs to be stripped out. This is very calculated and the maximum value a step value can have given the total number of bits.

$$\text{Step value} \;=\; 2\,(R+C)\;/\;\text{Total bits}$$

$$\text{Perimeter} \;=\; R+C+R+C \;=\; 2\,(R+C)$$

Figure 8 Step Formulation

Step size does not need to use this value, it

can be any number less than the maximum value, but it will compromise the effectiveness. Similarly, the process does not need to follow this way of calculating the step size. Any mathematical computation will work, as long as it could hide the total bits inside the perimeter of the image. Step size is a value by which the algorithm will traverse the pixels. Furthermore, it is a value that keeps enough distance between two-bit values, so that even if compression occurs, the value can still be recovered.

3.2 Advantages

- As the stored values represent the frequency and not the data bit, therefore, it decreases the effect of any compression on the payload.

- Gives the scope of improvements in spatial domain methods, due to the introduction of frequency instead of data itself.

- Without the starting point, and step size, it is difficult to reverse the process.

- Even though the rise in suspicion, cracking this steganography is still difficult.

3.3   Drawbacks

- Very less amount of data can be stored. Each byte requires at least 8 pixels.

- Visually distorted and can be observed with the native eye.

- Very complex to understand.

- Calculation of step size is a very tedious and challenging task

CHAPTER – 4 ALPHA

A pixel comprises 3 values which are red, green and blue. There is another field that plays a very promising role in the image structure, that is the Alpha value. The value of alpha controls the opacity factor in the image, and it ranges between 0-255. The value 255 means totally opaque and 0 means totally transparent. In this chapter, a very unique process of using alpha is discussed, and this is another prime focus of this book. The aim of the discussed method is to store an entire character inside a single pixel using alpha. In this technique, the entire cover image is affected because of a change in opacity level of each and every pixel, but it dramatically increases the payload capacity. It is very important to note that this technique is all about understanding the values and resources we have and how to use them properly while implementing any solution. It is a very standard mathematical computation but can be extended to any level of complexity until it follows the algorithmic standards.

4.1   Character Encoding

Let there be an image with entire white background of 'R' rows and 'C' columns. A pixel in this image would have red, green, blue and alpha values of 255 each. Let 'D' be a character to hide inside this pixel. Firstly, convert this character into its ASCII value, which in this case would be 100. According to the rule table, any ASCII character lies between the range of 0-255. Therefore, now we have a place to store this secret character in its ASCII value. Replace this ASCII value of the character with the alpha value and continue this for all the characters in the secret message. In this approach, the maximum amount of data can be stored inside an image, but all the pixels that have secret messages would be distorted on opacity level.

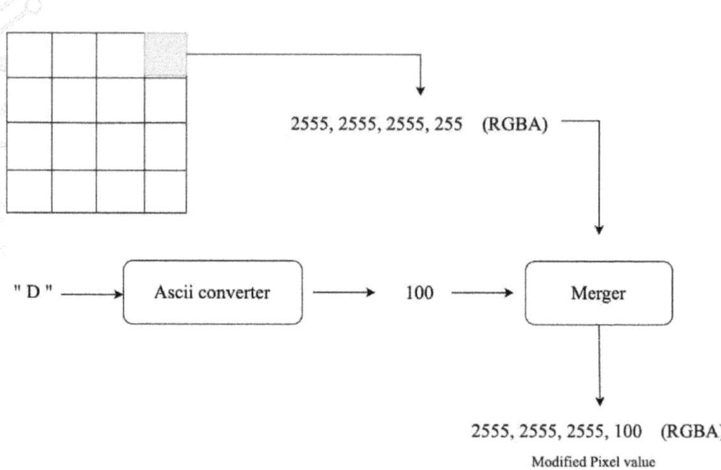

Figure 9 Alpha encryption model

Similarly, the secret message can be obtained as well. Firstly, the image is being processed and get the values of alpha from each pixel. The alpha value is then passed to a converter, which translates ASCII values to characters.

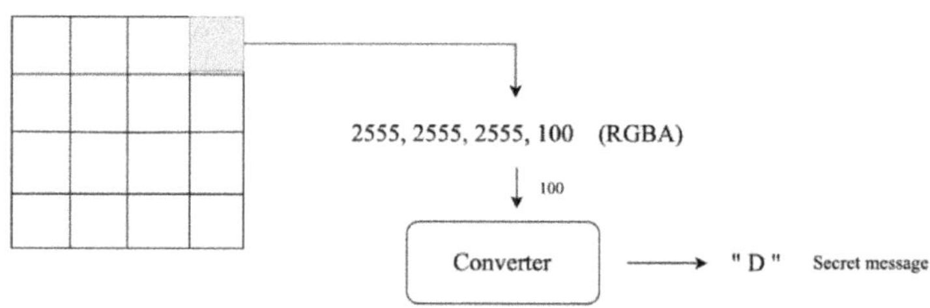

This technique summarizes the process of hiding character inside image using alpha values. Now, let's take this approach a bit further and try to hide images inside the image using the same approach.

4.2   Fusion

In this book "Dark Code" we're introducing a new term called Fusion, which is the process of hiding an image inside another image using alpha. The art of manipulating pixels to store data in such a way that the cover image does not get distorted is called steganography, but in this approach, the image is totally getting tampered with because of opacity manipulation. Therefore, we're calling it a fusion and the aim of this approach is to use the alpha value in a delightful way.

Grayscale Method

By using this algorithm, we can hide a grayscale image of equal dimensions as a cover image. The goal is to hide an entire pixel inside another pixel which is a very tedious task as manipulating the red, green, and blue values of a pixel to store the other red, green, and blue values sound difficult. Therefore, the main problem is how we can achieve this?

Firstly, apply the grayscale filter to the cover image. After this step, our problem is reduced to one-third, because now we have one value for red, green, and blue instead of three different values. From here on, we'll focus on hiding this value into alpha, and this is the same process that has been discussed in the Character Encoding section. The alpha value of a cover image is replaced by the pixel value of a grayscale image. The same process is applied to the entire image. Now, in order to retrieve this hidden image, reverse the entire process. Traverse through the image, and read the value of alpha. Place this value as red, green, and blue values of the decoded image. We have the hidden grayscale image.

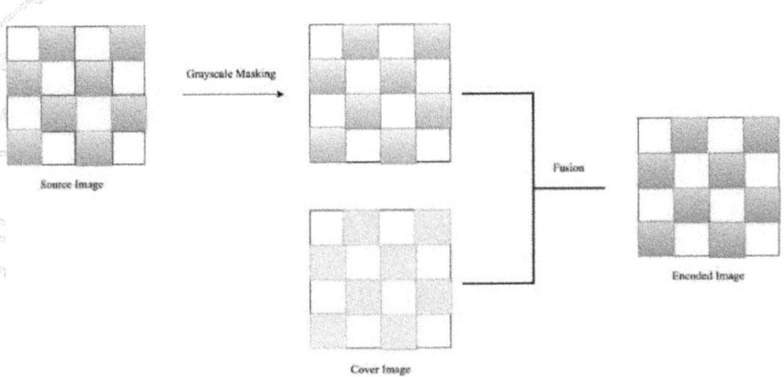

Figure 10 Grayscale Fusion

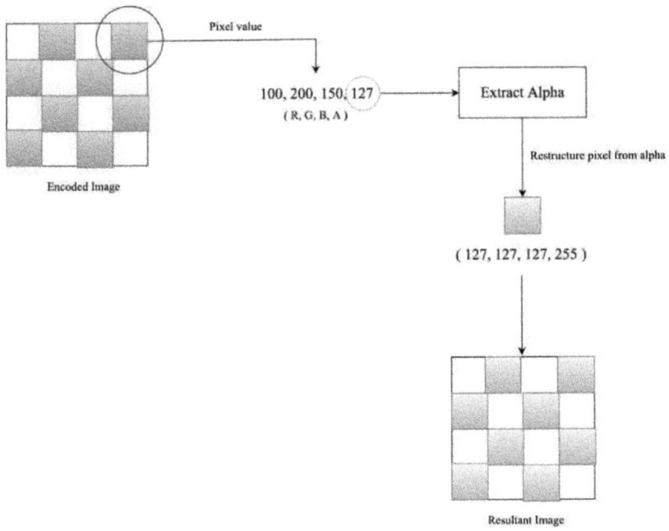

Figure 11 Reversing Fusion

Extension Method

This is an extension to the grayscale method. In the latter, it has been discussed that a way to store an entire pixel in another pixel is using alpha value. Similarly, this approach can also be used to store a coloured image inside another image. In this case, the approach remains the same, but with the slightest difference. Instead of applying a grayscale filter, values will be hidden natively. The technique follows a fact that there are three values to hide for a pixel that is red, green, and blue, and each pixel stores only a single value as per the Grayscale method. Therefore, 3 pixels from the cover image are required to store a single pixel from the secret image. Hence, the secret image has to be 1/3rd the size of the cover image for this method to work effectively.

Enhancement Points

- Alpha is a factor that controls the opacity of an image. In this chapter, only standards of playing with alpha are mentioned.

- These methods can be further enhanced to increase efficiency in terms of visual disorders.

- Extension method can only hide 1/3rd of an actual image. Work can be done to reduce this restriction.

- This chapter is totally dedicated to lossless and non-encrypted mediums, as alpha only works with steady formats, for example, PNG.

CHAPTER – 5 REFERENCES

1. Keshav Joshi, "A new approach of text steganography using ASCII values", International Journal of Engineering Research and Technology, Vol.7 Issue 05, May-2018, pp. 490-493.

2. Mehdi Hussain and Mureed Hussain, "A Survey of Image Steganography Techniques", International Journal of Advanced Science and Technology, Vol. 54, May-2013.

3. Vaishali P and Pradyumna Bhat, "Transform Domain Techniques of Image Steganography", International Journal of Innovative Research in Electrical, Electronics, Instrumentation and Control Engineering, Vol. 3, Special Issue 1, Apr-2015.

4. Tushara M, K.A. Navas, "Image Steganography Using Discrete Wavelet

Transform – A Review", International Journal of Innovative Research in Electrical, Electronics, Instrumentation and Control Engineering, Vol. 3, Special Issue 1, Feb-2016.

5. S. Islam, Mangat R. Modi, Phalguni Gupta, "Edge based Image Steganography", EURASIP Journal on Information Technology, Apr-2014

www.ingramcontent.com/pod-product-compliance
Ingram Content Group UK Ltd.
Pitfield, Milton Keynes, MK11 3LW, UK
UKHW041055250325
456693UK00001B/28

9 789390 724918